Our
San Diego

Photography by Ambient Images

Voyageur
Press

On the front cover: With the California Tower looming in the background, the Alcazar Garden in Balboa Park is based on the design of the Alcazar Castle Gardens in Seville, Spain. *Peter Bennett/California Stock Photo*

Page 1: Point Loma provides the perfect vantage point from which to view the beautiful San Diego skyline. In the foreground, on the banks of San Diego Bay, lie Shelter Island and the San Diego Yacht Club. *Peter Bennett/California Stock Photo*

Page 2: The world-famous Hotel del Coronado, one of America's most beautiful beach resorts, has hosted presidents and other notables such as Charles Lindberg and Babe Ruth. *Peter Bennett/California Stock Photo*

Page 3: Balboa Park's Alcazar Garden, known for its ornate fountains and Moorish tiles, contains more than 7,000 annuals planted each year to create the vibrant and vivid colors that line its paths. *Peter Bennett/California Stock Photo*

Page 4: A lone surfer catches a wave near day's end at Windansea Beach in La Jolla. The Windansea Surf Club was formed in 1962, and its several hundred members take part in surf competitions and also donate time and resources to the local community. *Peter Bennett/California Stock Photo*

Page 5, top: A child holds a starfish at Sea-World, one of San Diego's premier attractions. In addition to entertainment and family fun, SeaWorld also offers educational information and resources about the animals and our ecosystem. *Larry Brownstein/California Stock Photo*

Page 5, bottom: Dozens of flamingos flock near the entrance to the world-famous San Diego Zoo. Flamingos are social birds that can be found in colonies numbering in the thousands. *Peter Bennett/California Stock Photo*

Title page, main image: The San Diego skyline lights up as dusk settles on San Diego Bay and the hundreds of sailboats that dot its marinas. *Peter Bennett/California Stock Photo*

Title page, inset: In its early days, the bells of Mission San Diego de Alcalá were used to indicate when it was time to eat, pray, work, or play. Currently, all five bells are rung together only once a year, in commemoration of the birthday of the mission. *Peter Bennett/California Stock Photo*

On the back cover: (top) Flamingos at the San Diego Zoo. *Peter Bennett/California Stock Photo;* (center) Cliffs and beaches at La Jolla Cove. *Christopher T. Frank/California Stock Photo;* (bottom) Manchester Grand Hyatt and San Diego Marriott Hotel and Marina, on San Diego Bay. *Peter Bennett/California Stock Photo.*

The statue *Guardian of the Waters*, showing a pioneer woman holding a jug of water, stands outside the San Diego City and County Administration Building. Constructed in 1938, it was intended to be part of a larger complex of civic buildings overlooking the Embarcadero, but the other buildings were never built. *Peter Bennett/California Stock Photo*

ABOVE:

From a population of 18,000 at the turn of the last century, San Diego has exploded into one of our fastest growing cites, spawning the real estate boom of the last decade. Today's population has reached 1.23 million, with 3 million countywide. *Peter Bennett/California Stock Photo*

RIGHT:

Starting in the 1960s, modern
skyscrapers such as these near 6th
Avenue were sprouting up in
San Diego's growing downtown area.
Peter Bennett/California Stock Photo

ABOVE:

Built in 1863 on the Isle of Man and named *Euterpe*, the *Star of India* is now the flagship of the Maritime Museum of San Diego. It is the world's oldest active ship. *Peter Bennett/California Stock Photo*

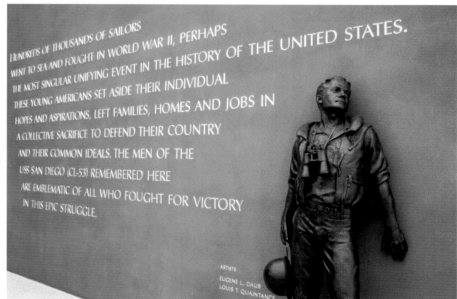

TOP:

Viewed here through the wheel of the *Star of India*, the HMS *Surprise* is a recent addition to the museum's fleet. It was purchased in 2004 from 20th Century Fox after being used in the Academy Award–winning film, *Master and Commander: The Far Side of the World. Peter Bennett/California Stock Photo*

BOTTOM:

Sculptors Eugene Daub and Louis Quaintance designed this public artwork along Harbor Drive, commemorating the USS *San Diego* (CL-53) and her crew for their sacrifices and contributions during World War II. *Larry Brownstein/California Stock Photo*

ABOVE:

Sailors stand guard for the arrival of sailors and marines
from the *Bonhomme Richard*. *Peter Bennett/California
Stock Photo*

ABOVE:

The USS *Bonhomme Richard*, part of Expeditionary Strike Group 5, returns to California after a six-month deployment overseas in support of Operation Unified Assistance and Operation Iraqi Freedom. *Peter Bennett/California Stock Photo*

LEFT:
These sailors smile, wave, and chat on cell phones as they pull into the home port of San Diego. *Peter Bennett/ California Stock Photo*

ABOVE:

A young girl eagerly waits to welcome her daddy home. *Peter Bennett/California Stock Photo*

ABOVE:

It was a tearful and happy reunion for many families of sailors and marines on active duty. *Peter Bennett/California Stock Photo*

ABOVE:

Families pack the pier to greet the returning sailors and marines from the *Bonhomme Richard*.

Peter Bennett/California Stock Photo

ABOVE:
Seaport Village lies at the center of San Diego's flourishing waterfront and Embarcadero. Filled with shops, restaurants, musicians, and even a carousel, the village offers numerous distractions for its many yearly visitors.
Peter Bennett/California Stock Photo

TOP:

Fog clouds the view from this dockside restaurant at Seaport Village overlooking San Diego Bay and the long span of the San Diego–Coronado Bridge in the background. *Peter Bennett/California Stock Photo*

BOTTOM:

Part of the Port of San Diego's Public Art Program, the sculpture *Surfboard Cedar Survivor* lines the waterfront Embarcadero, along with many other works in the "Urban Trees" project. *Peter Bennett/California Stock Photo*

ABOVE:

Located on eleven acres along San Diego Bay, the San Diego Convention Center opened its doors in 1989 and expanded to its present size in 2001. Its many outdoor terraces, airy indoor spaces, and breathtaking views help rank it among the top convention facilities in North America. *Peter Bennett/California Stock Photo*

OPPOSITE PAGE:

PETCO Park plays peek-a-boo behind Niki de Saint Phalle's public art sculpture, *Coming Together*. Standing thirty-eight feet tall and located next to the Convention Center, the sculpture is a ceramic and mirror mosaic that represents the duality of self. *Peter Bennett/California Stock Photo*

Located in the heart of downtown, PETCO Park, home of the San Diego Padres, is a beautiful example of a modern ballpark. It provides state-of-the-art facilities while incorporating the older surrounding buildings into its design, most notably the 1909 Western Metal Supply Company Building in the left-field corner. *Peter Bennett/ California Stock Photo*

TOP:

John D. Spreckels, a prominent San Diego businessman and philanthropist of the late 1800s and early 1900s, commissioned architect Harrison Albright to build the Spreckels Theatre in 1912. The first modern commercial playhouse west of the Mississippi, it has been staging shows for over ninety years at its downtown Broadway address. *Peter Bennett/California Stock Photo*

BOTTOM:

The Gaslamp Quarter is a mélange of architectural styles in the heart of the city. Originally intended to be the main business district, it has undergone many changes over the years, including names (such as Flea Town and Rabbitville), and has been home to such luminaries as Wyatt Earp and the notorious madam Ida Bailey. The quarter is currently the center of San Diego nightlife. *Peter Bennett/California Stock Photo*

OPPOSITE PAGE:

Jahja Ling is the conductor of the San Diego Symphony Orchestra at Copley Hall, originally built in 1929 as the Fox Theatre, a movie theater and office complex. In 1985, a $6-million renovation project restored the theater and its pipe organ. *Peter Bennett/California Stock Photo*

Under the supervision of owner Ulysses S. Grant Jr., the U.S. Grant Hotel opened its doors in 1910 on Broadway and quickly became an internationally celebrated hotel. It is undergoing a $48-million renovation. *Peter Bennett/California Stock Photo*

Although it currently resides on the concourse of the Horton Plaza shopping development, the Jessop Clock has been a fixture in San Diego since 1907. It has had several homes in front of J. Jessop and Sons jewelry store, won awards at the state fair, and even had a poem written about it, entitled "Jessop's Clock." *Peter Bennett/ California Stock Photo*

Named after Alonzo Erastus Horton, the man responsible for the development of modern San Diego, Horton Plaza encompasses more than six blocks and seven levels. The Plaza consists of colorful and sometimes quirky architecture, and its corridors twist through dozens of shops, restaurants, boutiques, and theaters. *Peter Bennett/California Stock Photo*

TOP:

A San Diego Trolley speeds past the Spanish Mission-Colonial Revival style Santa Fe Depot. Originally built in 1915 for the Panama-California International Exposition celebrating the opening of the Panama Canal, the station lies at the north end of Broadway near the Embarcadero. *Peter Bennett/California Stock Photo*

BOTTOM:

The station's interior walls are bordered by eight-and-a-half-foot-high, Moorish-style glazed tile wainscoting ornamented with the insignia of the Santa Fe Railroad. *Peter Bennett/California Stock Photo*

ABOVE:

The depot's waiting room, still in active use for Amtrak's Coaster Commuter train, features sixteen bronze-and-glass chandeliers, soft oak benches, and steam-heat radiators. *Peter Bennett/California Stock Photo*

In addition to the San Diego Zoo, Balboa Park is home to fifteen museums originally constructed for the 1915 Panama-California Exposition. A statue of El Cid stands in front of the House of Hospitality, which houses many of the park's offices as well as its visitor's center and the Prado Restaurant. *Peter Bennett/California Stock Photo*

BELOW:

Jonathon Borofsky's *Hammering Man at 3,110,527* greets visitors to the Museum of Contemporary Art, located across from the Santa Fe Depot and next to the main trolley station. *Peter Bennett/California Stock Photo*

LEFT:

Built in the Spanish Colonial style, the Museum of Man façade features representations of prominent figures from San Diego history. *Peter Bennett/California Stock Photo*

OPPOSITE PAGE:

The Museum of Man, located on El Prado in Balboa Park, is an anthropological museum with collections on Mayan culture, ancient Egypt, the Kumeyaay Indians of San Diego County, Human Evolution, and the Human Life Cycle. The one-hundred-bell carillon in the California Tower rings every quarter hour. *Peter Bennett/California Stock Photo*

ABOVE:

Balboa Park's San Diego Automotive Museum opened its doors in December 1988 and its collection of vintage cars, like this 1950s Oldsmobile, has been bringing back fond memories ever since. *Peter Bennett/California Stock Photo*

OPPOSITE PAGE TOP:

A Convair YF2Y-1 Sea Dart dramatically guards the entrance of the San Diego Aerospace Museum in Balboa Park. More than sixty-eight full-sized aircraft somehow inhabit the museum, built in the Streamlined Moderne architectural style. *Peter Bennett/California Stock Photo*

OPPOSITE PAGE BOTTOM:

Visitors can take a simulated walk in space or see the Apollo 9 Command Module, but the hit of the Aerospace museum is the Wright Flyer Simulator, which allows visitors to experience what it felt like when Orville and Wilbur Wright made their historic flight at Kitty Hawk in 1903. *Peter Bennett/California Stock Photo*

ABOVE:

The Bea Evenson Memorial Fountain is located at the eastern hub of El Prado next to the
Natural History Museum. It's a nice spot to rest one's feet, cool off, and perhaps listen to some
tunes performed by local buskers. *Richard Carroll/California Stock Photo*

ABOVE:

A didgeridoo player entertains passersby along El Prado on a Sunday afternoon in Balboa Park. A variety of jugglers, musicians, and other street entertainers can be found performing at the park on weekends. *Peter Bennett/California Stock Photo*

ABOVE:

The San Diego Lawn Bowling Club was formed in 1931 and has over a hundred members today.
Free lessons are available to those interested, but you might want to wear white, the official dress code
of the club. *Peter Bennett/California Stock Photo*

LEFT:

Perhaps dreaming of waves past, a
visitor to the Hall of Champions
views the Surfing Legends exhibit.
You can also find displays of
local heroes from baseball, football,
fishing, and many other sports.
Peter Bennett/California Stock Photo

RIGHT:

French-born artist Niki de Saint
Phalle's whimsical mosaic-type
sculpture of basketball players adorns
the front lawn of the San Diego Hall
of Champions Sports Museum. *Peter
Bennett/California Stock Photo*

The San Diego Zoo is dedicated to protecting and celebrating our natural world through education and conservation, and it is a popular destination for kids and adults alike. Within the zoo's one hundred acres can be found some four thousand animals of all shapes and sizes. *Peter Bennett/ California Stock Photo (opposite page top, this page top left and top right); Bill Lies/California Stock Photo (opposite page bottom); Larry Brownstein/California Stock Photo (this page bottom left and bottom right)*

ABOVE:

Built in 1905 by local architects William Hebbard and Irving Gill, the Marston House was the home of George Marston, a San Diego merchant, philanthropist, and civic leader. The interior design reflects the style of the American Arts and Crafts Movement. *Peter Bennett/ California Stock Photo*

OPPOSITE PAGE:

This is one of many stately mansions that line Banker's Hill, an uptown neighborhood that was a magnet for wealthy financiers and other prominent San Diegans at the turn of the last century. *Peter Bennett/California Stock Photo*

RIGHT:

Heritage Park, located across from Old Town Historic Park, is home to several beautifully preserved Victorian houses that were saved from demolition during the post–World War II expansion of downtown San Diego. *Peter Bennett/California Stock Photo*

ABOVE:

Because of its convenient trolley connection to downtown, Hillcrest was one of the city's earliest suburbs. Today its streets are lined with bookstores, coffee houses, theaters, and restaurants. Hillcrest is also the heart of San Diego's gay community. *Peter Bennett/California Stock Photo*

LEFT:
Two docents pose
in front of Casa
de Estudillo
at Old Town State
Historic Park,
where the city
of San Diego first
began. The
Estudillo adobe,
built around a
garden courtyard,
was constructed
in 1827 and
restored in 1910.
*Peter Bennett/
California Stock
Photo*

RIGHT:
Old Town park re-creates California
life in the Mexican and early
American periods of 1821 to 1872.
The settlement includes five original
adobes, a schoolhouse, a blacksmith's
shop, and California's first newspaper
office. *Peter Bennett/California Stock
Photo*

Although construction of Interstate 5 and the San Diego–Coronado Bridge dislocated much of the population in the 1960s, Barrio Logan remains a centerpiece of the city's Mexican-American community. Murals throughout the neighborhood celebrate Mexican and Chicano history and culture. *Larry Brownstein/California Stock Photo*

Designated a city historic site in 1980, Chicano Park contains murals by nearly every major Chicano muralist of the 1970s and early 1980s. The park and its murals, which are painted directly on the concrete pylons of the Coronado Bridge, were a response to the devastating effects of the bridge's construction on Barrio Logan. *Peter Bennett/California Stock Photo*

Opened in 1969, the San Diego–Coronado Bridge connects mainland San Diego with Coronado Island across San Diego Bay. The orthotropic design and sweeping, ninety-degree mid-span curve make it possible for an empty aircraft carrier to pass underneath. *Peter Bennett/California Stock Photo*

ABOVE:

The turret atop the Hotel del Coronado glows warmly as dusk settles in and guests sip cocktails or walk on the beautiful white beaches of Coronado Island. The resort may be best known as the setting of the classic 1959 movie *Some Like It Hot*, starring Marilyn Monroe, Tony Curtis, and Jack Lemmon. *Peter Bennett/California Stock Photo*

ABOVE:

The foot of Orange Avenue at Coronado Island's Ferry Landing Marketplace leads to a vibrant commercial district containing restaurants and cafés, theaters, boutiques, and Coronado's Museum of History and Art. *Peter Bennett/ California Stock Photo*

LEFT:

The Art Deco entrance of the MooTime Creamery on Orange Avenue is flanked by statues of a cow and "The King." *Peter Bennett/California Stock Photo*

TOP:

With the Imperial Beach Fishing Pier in the background, a couple enjoys the surf and sun at one of San Diego's most popular beaches. *Larry Brownstein/California Stock Photo*

BOTTOM:

Throngs of visitors are drawn to the annual U.S. Open Sandcastle Competition at Imperial Beach, a three-day event held every July. Dozens of sand castles line the beach, with both amateurs and professionals alike competing for thousands of dollars in prize money. *Larry Brownstein/ California Stock Photo*

ABOVE:

Intricate artworks such as these are on display at the U.S. Open Sandcastle Competition. Viewing the carvings during the competition's official hours is recommended, otherwise they may be washed away by the incoming tides. *Larry Brownstein/California Stock Photo*

This braided, tattooed beachgoer at Imperial Beach follows that old Southern California weekend custom of showing off your stuff. *Larry Brownstein/California Stock Photo*

ABOVE:

The Tunaman's Memorial on Shelter Island was created by artist/fisherman Franco Vianello out of bronze in 1988. The sculpture honors the Italian, Japanese, Portuguese, and Slavic fishermen who constituted the once-large tuna industry operating out of San Diego Bay. *Peter Bennett/ California Stock Photo*

LEFT:

The Naval Air Station on Coronado Island is just visible through the early morning fog as fishermen try their luck from a Shelter Island fishing pier. *Peter Bennett/California Stock Photo*

ABOVE:

The Old Point Loma Lighthouse, part of Cabrillo National Monument, stands 422 feet above sea level. It had a short life as guardian of San Diego Bay from 1855 to 1891. *Bill Lies/California Stock Photo*

LEFT:

More than eighty-five thousand veterans are buried in Fort Rosecrans National Cemetery's seventy-seven acres on Point Loma. Along with a majestic view of the bay, the cemetery boasts several monuments, including to the Mexican-American War's Battle of San Pasqual and to the sixty-two lives lost on the USS *Bennington* when the ship's boiler exploded in San Diego harbor in 1905. *Peter Bennett/California Stock Photo*

ABOVE:

Juan Rodríguez Cabrillo, sailing under the flag of Spain, was in search of riches and a northern route connecting the Pacific and Atlantic oceans when he reached San Diego while sailing north from the Mexican coast. This monument at the end of Point Loma was created in 1913. *Peter Bennett/California Stock Photo*

ABOVE:

The arrival of Juan Rodríguez Cabrillo's ship, the *San Salvador*, in California is re-enacted in San Diego Bay during the Cabrillo Festival every October. Cabrillo landed at Ballast Point on Point Loma in 1542. *Peter Bennett/California Stock Photo*

OPPOSITE PAGE:

Visitors to the Cabrillo Festival can watch docents in sixteenth-century costume demonstrate weapons and armor, knot tying, and other period re-creations. *Peter Bennett/California Stock Photo*

Tide-pooling is a popular activity along the ocean side of Point Loma. Observers can view a multitude of animal and plant sea life amidst the coastline's fragile intertidal ecosystem. *Peter Bennett/California Stock Photo*

ABOVE:

Mission Beach is a two-mile peninsula that stretches from Mission Bay Channel, just north of Ocean Beach, to Pacific Beach. The Ocean Front Walk is a great way to see the sights, be it by foot, bike, skateboard, or inline skates. *Peter Bennett/California Stock Photo*

RIGHT:

Dozens of happy, leash-free dogs can be found jumping and running through the surf at Dog Beach at the northern end of Ocean Beach. Here, dogs rule and masters follow. *Peter Bennett/California Stock Photo*

ABOVE:

Mission Bay Park is the largest man-made aquatic park in the country. It encompasses 4,235 acres of waterways, playgrounds, bike paths, and open fields. In 1944 the city government, in an effort to attract tourism, began transforming a tidal marsh originally named "False Bay" into the park it is today. *Peter Bennett/California Stock Photo*

Weekends find San Diegans flocking to Mission Bay Park for fun and activity on both land and water. Jet-skiers, joggers, bikers, and rollerbladers fill the pathways and waterways throughout the park. *Peter Bennett/California Stock Photo*

BELOW:

Fiesta Island, located in the middle of Mission Bay, offers colorful springtime strolls through acres and acres of wildflowers. The island is also a popular launching spot for recreational water sports such as water-skiing and jet-skiing. *Peter Bennett/California Stock Photo*

LEFT:
Kite flying is another popular, if less strenuous, activity at Mission Bay Park, as is simply sitting on the grass and enjoying the cool ocean breezes. *Peter Bennett/California Stock Photo*

BELOW:
The San Diego Crew Classic is held every spring at Crown Point Shores Park in Mission Bay. The event was established in 1973 by two of San Diego's premier rowing clubs, and today schools from all over the country come here to compete in one of the most distinguished rowing competitions in the world. *Larry Brownstein/California Stock Photo*

LEFT:
Shamu, the world-famous killer whale, and a family member perform at SeaWorld. Audience members in the front rows are sure to get soaked. *Larry Brownstein/ California Stock Photo*

ABOVE:

The Coaster Saloon, named for its proximity to Belmont Park, is a self-proclaimed dive that attracts bikers and beachgoers alike. *Larry Brownstein/California Stock Photo*

Chaos is one of the many exhilarating rides at Mission Beach's Belmont Park. The park opened in 1925 as the Mission Beach Amusement Center. Its main attraction was the Giant Dipper roller coaster, visible here behind the spinning lights of Chaos. *Larry Brownstein/California Stock Photo*

Funhouse Tattoos and Body Piercing offers adventurous customers a variety of styles and designs from its location in the heart of Mission Beach. *Larry Brownstein/California Stock Photo*

The Crystal Pier
Hotel is unique
in that its
Cape Cod–style
cottages line the
pier directly
over the beach
and ocean. The
pier was built
in 1927, but the
blue-shuttered
cottages and
hotel were not
added until 1936.
Peter Bennett/
California Stock
Photo

ABOVE:

Another perfect San Diego sunset, as strollers catch the last rays at the end of the Crystal Pier in Pacific Beach. *Larry Brownstein/California Stock Photo*

ABOVE:

If you need to rent a bike or surfboard, or just get some great beach gear, Hamel's Surf and Skate is one of many shops in Mission Beach that can help you out. *Peter Bennett/California Stock Photo*

ABOVE:

Surfing is the favored pastime all along San Diego's coastline. *Richard Carroll/California Stock Photo*

TOP:

Tourmaline Surfing Park, at the northern end of Pacific Beach, offers some of the best breaks and surfing around. Rich in surfing tradition, locals and old timers can often be found in the parking lot catching up and dispensing lore. *Peter Bennett/California Stock Photo*

BOTTOM:

Ocean Beach Municipal Pier is a great place to catch some waves—or to catch those catching the waves. The pier extends a half mile offshore. *Peter Bennett/ California Stock Photo*

ABOVE:

A yellow surfboard juxtaposed against a mural at
Tourmaline Surfing Park creates a beautiful and tranquil
post-surfing moment. *Larry Brownstein/California
Stock Photo*

LEFT:

On land, San Diegans take to a different form of boarding. The Coronado Skatepark, located at Tidelands Park in the shadow of the Coronado Bridge, features two large bowls and a street course. *Peter Bennett/California Stock Photo*

BELOW:

Windansea Beach's rocky coastline, sloping cliffs, and undersea reefs create the perfect spot for surfers looking for a secluded beach with great surf breaks. Its landmark grass hut has been standing since the 1940s. *Peter Bennett/California Stock Photo*

La Jolla Cove is a picturesque beach popular with bathers, snorkelers, and scuba divers. It is located within the San Diego La Jolla Underwater Park Ecological Reserve, which preserves native marine plants and animals in their natural state. *Peter Bennett/ California Stock Photo*

ABOVE:

The Grande Colonial opened for business in 1913, originally charging $1 a room. The early 1900s brought many institutions to the area, including the Scripps Institution of Oceanography, and the hotel catered to visitors of the burgeoning community. *Peter Bennett/California Stock Photo*

OPPOSITE PAGE:

La Jolla's La Valencia Hotel, a beautiful example of Mediterranean design with views to match, was built in 1926 and has hosted a long list of the rich and famous. The tiered gardens of the "Pink Lady" extend down to La Jolla Cove. *Peter Bennett/California Stock Photo*

ABOVE:

A little bit Mediterranean, a little bit Beverly Hills, La Jolla is one of our most affluent communities. Its streets are lined with fine restaurants, art galleries, and fashionable boutiques such as this one on Girard Street. *Peter Bennett/ California Stock Photo*

ABOVE:

Mount Soledad Memorial Cross was erected in 1954 to honor the veterans of the Korean War. In recent years, controversy has been brewing about whether the cross violates the separation of church and state. *Peter Bennett/California Stock Photo*

RIGHT:

More than eight hundred feet above sea level, Mount Soledad offers spectacular 360-degree views of La Jolla's seventeen miles of coastline and the surrounding area. *Peter Bennett/California Stock Photo*

OPPOSITE PAGE:

Torrey Pines State Reserve covers more than two thousand acres and is home to the rare Torrey pine. Broken Hill Trail is part of eight miles of trails with dramatic coastal views and guided nature walks. *Anthony Arendt/California Stock Photo*

ABOVE:

Low tide exposes the many tide pools that thrive with marine animal and plant life along La Jolla's coastline. *Christopher T. Frank/California Stock Photo*

LEFT:
Brown pelicans perch on the rocks near La Jolla Cove. The banning of many pesticides has helped this endangered bird species make a comeback. These beautiful birds have wingspans of up to seven feet.
Richard Carroll/California Stock Photo

ABOVE:
The Scripps Institution of Oceanography Research Pier juts out into the Pacific at the northern end of La Jolla. The institute is one of the foremost centers for ocean research and marine science, attracting scientists and students from around the world. *Peter Bennett/California Stock Photo*

Birch Aquarium at Scripps is a great place for kids and families to learn about marine life. Exhibits include outdoor tide-pool displays, the Hall of Fishes and Shark Reef, the underwater Simulator Ride, and a learning center featuring workshops and classes. *Peter Bennett/California Stock Photo*

A statue of a gray whale greets visitors to the Birch Aquarium at Scripps. *Peter Bennett/California Stock Photo*

Hope lies in dreams, in imagination and in the courage of those who dare to make dreams into reality.

Jonas Salk

OPPOSITE PAGE:
Resembling a large UFO, the Geisel Library on the University of California, San Diego, campus is named for Audrey and Theodor Geisel and was designed by architect William L. Pereira, best known for designing the Transamerica Building in San Francisco. Theodor Geisel is famous for his works *The Cat in the Hat* and *Green Eggs and Ham*—written under his more familiar penname of Dr. Seuss. *Peter Bennett/California Stock Photo*

TOP:

Jonas Salk founded the Salk Institute for Biological Studies in 1962. Located on La Jolla's coastal cliffs, the institute works to increase our understanding of human health, concentrating on the study of molecular biology, genetics, and the neurosciences, as well as plant biology, with an eye toward improving the world's food supply. *Peter Bennett/California Stock Photo*

BOTTOM:

The University of California, San Diego, opened its campus doors in 1960 and is now a premier university. Its graduates and faculty are an integral part of the Golden Triangle's many scientific institutions and corporations. *Peter Bennett/California Stock Photo*

Operated by the California Institute of Technology,
Palomar Observatory is home to the two-hundred-inch
Hale Telescope, until 1993 the world's largest
optical telescope. The observatory is in northern
San Diego County, 5,500 feet above sea level on Mount
Palomar. *Anthony Arendt/California Stock Photo*

A father and son stroll on South Carlsbad State Beach, which features a popular campground situated right along the bluffs. *Peter Bennett/California Stock Photo*

LEFT:

No, a photo of San Francisco hasn't slipped into this book. That's the Legoland version of the city by the bay. *Larry Brownstein/California Stock Photo*

ABOVE:

Legoland, located in Carlsbad, is a theme park based on the popular building blocks. Among the park's attractions is Miniland USA, a miniature reproduction of seven locations, such as New York City, each comprised of more than twenty million Lego bricks. *Larry Brownstein/ California Stock Photo*

LEFT:

New Orleans' French Quarter is another Legoland attraction. *Larry Brownstein/California Stock Photo*

It doesn't get more colorful than the ranunculus fields of Carlsbad in springtime. For six to eight weeks, from early March to May, the Flower Fields at Carlsbad Ranch blossom in a rainbow of color and enchant the more than 150,000 visitors who come to view the colorful displays. *Larry Brownstein/California Stock Photo*

A young girl sports a spring bonnet at the Carlsbad Flower Fields. There are fifty acres of rolling hills and bands of colorful flowers to enjoy and relax in. *Larry Brownstein/ California Stock Photo*

OPPOSITE PAGE:

Anza-Borrego Desert State Park is a popular destination for wildflower watchers from January through April. Here a purple carpet of sand verbena flowers covers the desert floor. *Thomas Hallstein/California Stock Photo*

ABOVE:

Hedgehog and barrel cacti bloom in the spring. In 2005, the heavy rains of the previous winter brought about one of the best desert bloom seasons in years. *Christopher T. Frank/California Stock Photo*

Anza-Borrego Desert State Park is the largest state park in the continental U.S., consisting of over 600,000 acres. Desert colors are on vibrant display in this sunset shot of an ocotillo plant, with Indian Head Peak in the background. *Anthony Arendt/ California Stock Photo*

Font's Point offers some of the most dramatic vistas in the desert park. The corrugated landscape changes shape and color as the sun sweeps across the Borrego Badlands. *Thomas Hallstein/California Stock Photo*

Another view from Font's Point shows the subtle shifts in light and color over the Colorado Desert. *Anthony Arendt/California Stock Photo*

ABOVE:

The "Lone Palm Tree" stands guard at Anza-Borrego's Una Palma Oasis. *Thomas Hallstein/California Stock Photo*

TOP:

The cracked earth in Font's Wash indicates where a small pool of water once lay. Rain pouring down the canyons can bring severe flash floods reaching heights of several feet. *Anthony Arendt/California Stock Photo*

BOTTOM:

Just forty miles east of downtown, Cuyamaca Rancho State Park and its twenty-six thousand acres of woodland forest is an easy trip for San Diegans looking for a little hiking, mountain biking, or camping. *Christopher T. Frank/California Stock Photo*

TOP:

Balloon trips are a spectacular way to tour the Temecula Valley wineries and view the rolling countryside, such as these orange groves. Every year the Temecula Valley Balloon and Wine Festival attracts thousands for balloon rides, wine tasting, and musical entertainment. *Richard Carroll/California Stock Photo*

BOTTOM:

The Ponte Family Estate Winery is one of twenty-one wineries, many family owned, in the Temecula Valley. The verdant vineyards and award-winning wines make the valley a popular destination for visitors from both San Diego and Los Angeles. *Thomas Hallstein/California Stock Photo*

ABOVE:

In fourth grade, California students are taught about social science and the state's history. Class trips are a vital part of the curriculum, and a visit to the Mission San Diego de Alcala is essential. *Peter Bennett/California Stock Photo*

Mission Basilica San Diego de Alcala was the first of the great California missions. Founded in 1769, the mission was rebuilt in 1931 and remains a spiritual, cultural, and historical center for the community. *Peter Bennett/California Stock Photo*

ABOVE:

This interior of the church at Mission San Diego de Alcala was part of the 1931 rebuild. Native Americans burned the original mission to the ground in 1775, and the property was used in several capacities before the mission was rebuilt. *Peter Bennett/California Stock Photo*

ABOVE:

Father Junipero Serra (1713–1784) was sent to establish Spanish rights to California and convert the Native Americans to Christianity. This statue of the five-foot-two-inch-tall, 120-pound padre is located at Mission San Diego de Alcala, the first of nine missions he founded along the seven-hundred-mile-long El Camino Real from San Diego to Sonoma. *Peter Bennett/California Stock Photo*

ABOVE:

Mission Santa Ysabel was established in 1818, dubbed the "Church of the Desert." It was intended as an *asistencia* to Mission San Diego, meaning it had a chapel but no resident missionary priest.
Thomas Hallstein/California Stock Photo

110

Mission San Luis Rey in Oceanside, once called the "King of the Missions," is the largest of the California missions. It was established in 1798, and the current structure was completed in 1815.

Larry Brownstein/California Stock Photo

Sunset Cliffs is the perfect place to watch another beautiful
San Diego day come to an end. *Christopher T. Frank/
California Stock Photo*